Marie Curie

by Dana Meachen Rau

Compass Point Early Biographies

Content Adviser: Professor Sherry L. Field,
Department of Social Science Education, College of Education,
The University of Georgia

Reading Adviser: Dr. Linda D. Labbo,
Department of Reading Education, College of Education,
The University of Georgia

COMPASS POINT BOOKS

Minneapolis, Minnesota

Compass Point Books
3109 West 50th Street, #115
Minneapolis, MN 55410

Visit Compass Point Books on the Internet at *www.compasspointbooks.com* or e-mail your request to *custserv@compasspointbooks.com*

Editors: E. Russell Primm and Emily J. Dolbear
Photo Researcher: Svetlana Zhurkina
Photo Selector: Dawn Friedman
Design: Bradfordesign, Inc.

Library of Congress Cataloging-in-Publication Data
Rau, Dana Meachen, 1971–
    Marie Curie / by Dana Meachen Rau.
        p. cm.—(Compass point early biographies)
    Includes bibliographical references and index.
    Summary: A brief biography of the scientist who twice received the Nobel Prize for her work with radium.
        ISBN 0-7565-0017-6 (hardcover : lib. bdg.)
        1. Curie, Marie, 1867–1934—Juvenile literature. 2. Chemists—Poland—Biography—Juvenile literature. [1. Curie, Marie, 1867–1934. 2. Chemists. 3. Women—Biography.] I. Title. II. Series.
    QD22.C8 R38 2000
    540'.92—dc21
                                                                        00-008668

38888000051726

Table of Contents

A Pioneer in Science

Marie Curie was a pioneer in science.
A pioneer is someone who does something
first and opens up new ideas to others.
Marie Curie discovered an **element**
called **radium**. She was the first woman
professor in France. She was also the first
woman to win a very important award, the
Nobel Prize—and she won it twice.

◄ Marie Curie in her laboratory

Young Manya

Marie spent most of her life in France, but her story begins in Poland. She was born as Maria Sklodowska on November 7, 1867. People called her Manya. She was the youngest of five children.

Manya and her sister Bronya

Manya's father was a professor of **physics** and math. School and science were important in her family. Manya did well in school, but her childhood was not always happy. Her father lost his job. When Manya was only eleven years old, her mother died.

Manya and her oldest sister, Bronya, wanted to go to the Sorbonne, France's best university. But the family did not have much money. Manya and Bronya decided to help each other. First, Manya got a job taking care of children. She sent the money she earned to Bronya to pay for her classes in Paris.

Marie at age
twenty-four
in Paris

Life in Paris

When Bronya finished her studies, she helped Manya. Manya left for Paris in 1891. She called herself Marie— French for Maria. In just three years, she got **degrees** in math and physics.

Pierre Curie

In Paris, Marie met a French scientist named Pierre Curie. He taught classes and ran a **laboratory**. A laboratory is a place where scientists work. Marie and Pierre fell in love. They were married on July 26, 1895.

Both of them loved learning about science.
They also enjoyed riding bicycles together.
A few years later, their first daughter, Irène,
was born.

Marie and Pierre with Irène ▲

◄ The Curies riding
bicycles on their
honeymoon

Science of the Time

At that time, many scientists were studying elements. Elements are basic substances that make up everything in nature. Marie was very interested in that kind of science.

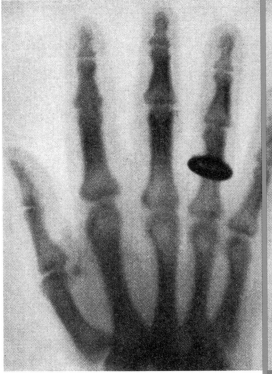

In 1895, a German scientist named Wilhelm Roentgen noticed rays of energy coming from some elements. He called them X rays. These rays could pass through soft objects,

An early X ray

Wilhelm Conrad Roentgen

11

such as skin. They did not pass through hard objects, such as bone. X rays could be used to take pictures of the human body to find broken bones and other problems. Then, a good friend of the Curies named Henri Becquerel found that an element called **uranium** gave off rays too.

One of the first X-ray machines

Marie in her lab ➤ in 1898

Studying Rays

Marie wanted to study these rays, but she needed a laboratory. At first, she worked in a small room at the Sorbonne. When she needed more space, all she could find was a shed with a dirt floor and leaky roof.

Marie found that only certain elements gave off **rays**—or **radioactivity**, as she called it. Then she started studying a brown or black **mineral** called **pitchblende**. She knew it had uranium in it. But pitchblende gave off so many rays that Marie thought it must contain more than one element. Pierre began to work with Marie.

Measuring radioactivity ➤

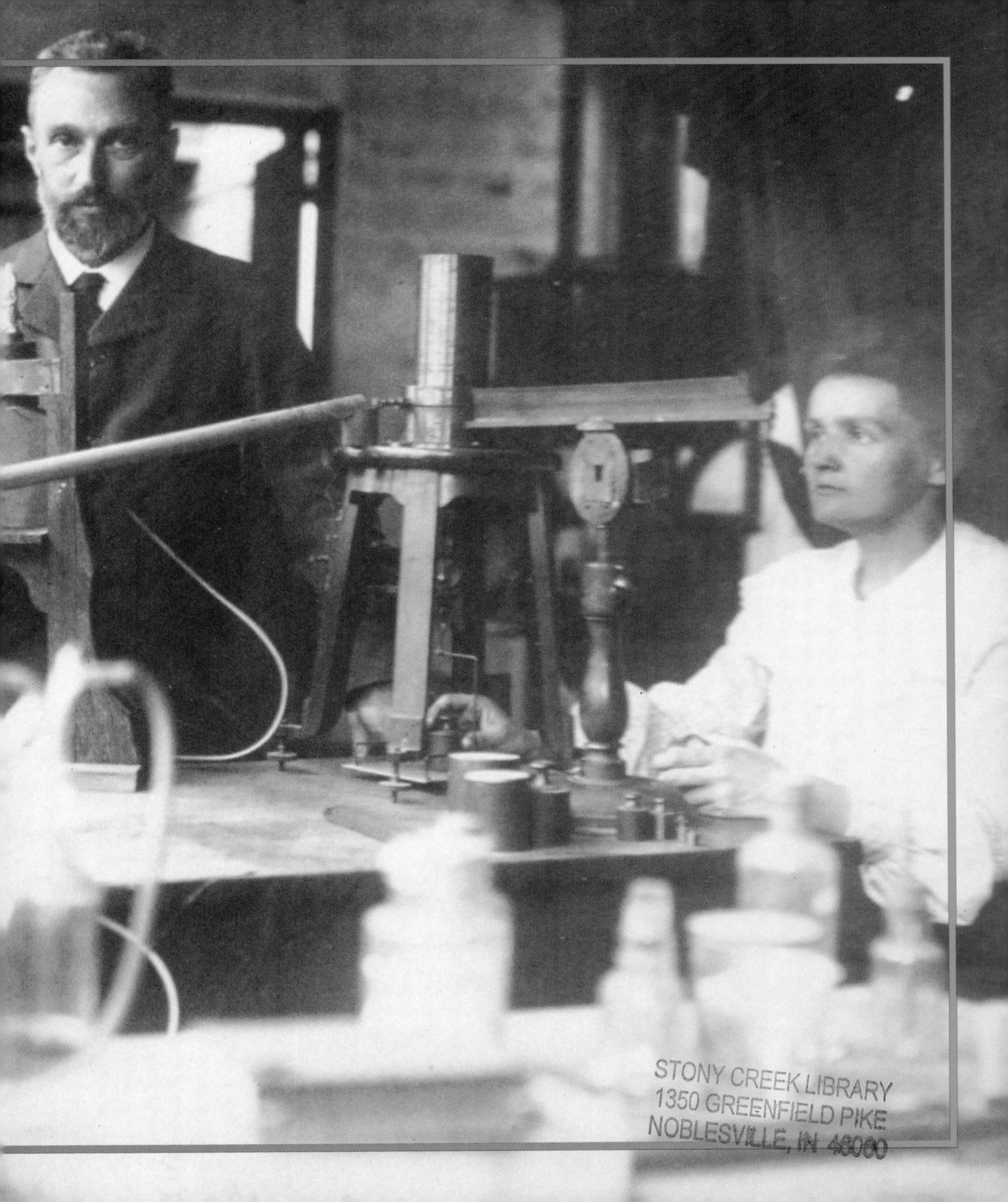

Finding New Elements

They found a new element. Marie called it **polonium**, after her homeland of Poland.

The Curies experimenting with radium

Then one night, Marie and Pierre saw a blue glow coming from their experiments. They had found another new element that gave off rays. Marie called it radium.

Radium was a very important element. Its radioactivity was two million times greater than that of uranium. It could be used in medicine to treat cancer. It could destroy unhealthy growths in the body called tumors.

Because radium was so powerful, it was also very harmful. Marie and Pierre worked with it so much that they suffered many illnesses. They had sores and blisters on their bodies. They often felt weak.

Successes

Soon Marie and Pierre Curie were famous. Scientists all over the world read about their discovery. Marie was given a doctor of science degree—the highest in the university. Then something more exciting happened. In 1903, Marie, Pierre, and their friend Henri won

Marie's Nobel Prize medal

the Nobel Prize for Physics. They received a gold medal and a large sum of money.

18

Pierre and Marie were thrilled to have money for their experiments—finally. Now

that they were famous, they were invited to fancy parties. But they were also very shy. Marie and Pierre preferred working in their laboratory.

The Curies were happy. Their second daughter, Eve,

Marie with Irène and Eve

was born in 1904. That year, Pierre became a professor of physics at the Sorbonne.

Marie and Pierre in the lab

An Accident

But in 1906, a terrible thing happened. Pierre
was hit by a horse-drawn wagon as he crossed
a busy street. He died instantly.

Marie missed Pierre very much. She kept
doing the work that they had always done
together. The
university gave
Pierre's job
to Marie. She
became the
first woman
professor at a
French university.

Pierre was killed by a horse-drawn wagon.

Marie taught at the Sorbonne. ➤

A Second Prize

Marie continued to study radioactivity. In 1911, she won a second Nobel Prize—this time, for chemistry. She was the first woman to win a Nobel Prize and the first person to win two Nobel Prizes.

The Radium Institute

Three years later, an organization for the study of radium called the Radium Institute was built. Marie gave it a very special gift—a gram of radium that she had prepared herself. It was the only gram of radium in France.

Marie talks to reporters. ➤

World War I and Fame

When France started fighting in World War I (1914–1918), Marie wanted to help the country. She set up an X-ray service for soldiers who had been hurt. It saved thousands of lives.

Marie holds the tube of radium given to her by U.S. president Warren Harding.

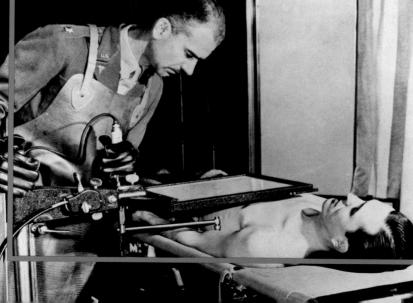

A portable X-ray machine

All over the world, people knew about Marie Curie. Women in the United States raised the money

Marie with her daughters in 1921

to buy another gram of radium for Marie's work. In 1921, Marie traveled to America to accept it. She was treated like a star.

Poland also built a radium institute called the Marie Sklodowska-Curie Institute. Again, Americans raised money for another gram of radium.

Irène Curie and her husband J. F. Joliot were also scientists.

An Important Life

Marie Curie's work helped the world and saved many lives. But her own body was weak from working with the harmful radium and X rays. In July 4, 1934, Marie died at the age of sixty-six.

But Marie Curie's amazing discoveries lived on. Her important work opened up the way for great progress in science and medicine.

◀ Marie Curie in later years

Important Dates in Marie Curie's Life

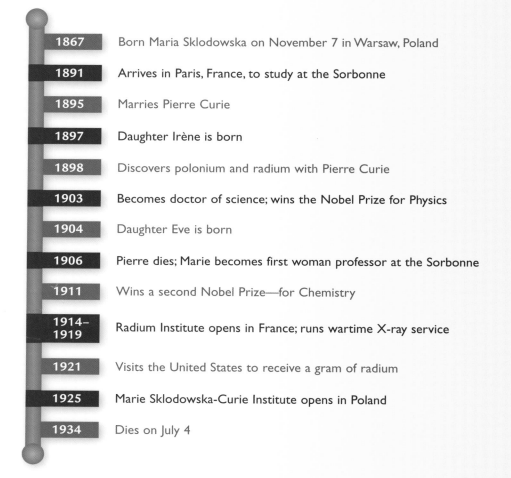

1867	Born Maria Sklodowska on November 7 in Warsaw, Poland
1891	Arrives in Paris, France, to study at the Sorbonne
1895	Marries Pierre Curie
1897	Daughter Irène is born
1898	Discovers polonium and radium with Pierre Curie
1903	Becomes doctor of science; wins the Nobel Prize for Physics
1904	Daughter Eve is born
1906	Pierre dies; Marie becomes first woman professor at the Sorbonne
1911	Wins a second Nobel Prize—for Chemistry
1914–1919	Radium Institute opens in France; runs wartime X-ray service
1921	Visits the United States to receive a gram of radium
1925	Marie Sklodowska-Curie Institute opens in Poland
1934	Dies on July 4

Glossary

element—one of several basic substances that make up everything in nature; a substance that cannot be split into a simpler substance

mineral—a substance found in nature that is not an animal or a plant

physics—the science of how energy affects things in nature

pitchblende—a mineral with that contains radium

polonium—an element with radioactivity found in pitchblende

radioactivity—the giving off of rays of energy

radium—an element with high levels of radioactivity

rays—beams of energy or light

uranium—an element with powerful radioactivity

Did You Know?

- Marie Curie had very little money as a student in Paris. She ate mostly bread, butter, and tea.

- Marie Curie was the first woman to be buried under the dome of the Panthéon in Paris in honor of her work. The Panthéon is a monument to French heroes.

- Marie Curie's daughter, Irène Joliot-Curie, won the Nobel Prize for Chemistry in 1935.

Want to Know More?

At the Library

Dunn, Andrew. *Marie Curie*. New York: Bookwright Press, 1991.
Tames, Richard. *Marie Curie*. New York: Franklin Watts, 1989.

On the Web

For more information on Marie Curie, use FactHound
to track down Web sites related to this book.

1. Go to *www.facthound.com*
2. Type in a search word related to this book
   or this book ID: 0756500176
3. Click on the *Fetch It* button.

Your trusty FactHound will fetch the best Web sites for you!

Through the Mail

Musée Curie (The Curie Museum)
11, rue Pierre et Marie Curie
75248 Paris CEDEX 05, France
For information about Marie Curie's work

On the Road

Fermi National Accelerator Laboratory
Kirk Road and Pine
Batavia, IL 60510
630 / 840-3000
For exhibits about the nature of matter

Index

About the Author

Ever since Dana Meachen Rau can remember, she has loved to write. A graduate of Trinity College in Hartford, Connecticut, Rau works as a children's book editor and illustrator and has written many books for children, including biographies, nonfiction, early readers, and historical fiction. Rau lives in Farmington, Connecticut, with her husband, Chris, and son, Charlie.